SEE WHAT OTHER READERS ON AMAZON HAVE TO SAY…

★ ★ ★ ★ ★

"This should be mandatory reading for all bosses. A great read. So many of these ideas seem to be common sense, but unfortunately common sense *isn't* common. Really highlights the pressures placed on managers to find the quickest, cheapest path to higher staff and the real costs involved in a bad hire. Will be sharing this gold!"

★ ★ ★ ★ ★

"A practical guide. Easy to read. An indispensable tool that will improve hiring decisions."

★ ★ ★ ★ ★

"If you're looking for sound, practical advice on hiring, this book provides it. Ken has shared a lifetime of learning on the subject to save readers making mistakes that most people make when hiring. Easy and interesting to read and even easier to successfully apply."

★ ★ ★ ★ ★

"A brilliant read. A clear and concise view into the hiring process. These insights will no doubt prove to be invaluable to any business owner or manager looking to find the right candidate and fit for their team."

★ ★ ★ ★ ★

"This is more than a book on recruitment. It highlights the importance of building competent and thriving teams to meet personal and organizational objectives. It describes how to influence those who place little value on these things. Another great resource from Dr Ken Byrne that I'll be referring to for many years to come."

★ ★ ★ ★ ★

"This book is clearly written, concise and specific. It contains checklists, anecdotes and explanations that are obviously based on a wealth of experience."

Seeing Behind the Job Applicant's Mask Before Hiring

Secrets of a Corporate Psychologist

Volume 1

By Dr. Ken Byrne

ISBN:9780648675501

DISCLAIMER
This book is designed to provide information and motivation to our readers. It is sold with the understanding that neither the author or publisher is not engaged to provide any type of legal, psychological or medical advice. The content of this book is the sole expression and opinion of the author, and not necessarily that of the publisher. No warranties or guarantees expressed or implied by the publisher's choice to include any of the content in this volume. Neither the publisher nor the individual author shall be liable for any physical, psychological, emotional, financial or commercial damages. This includes, but is not limited to, incidental, consequential or other damages. You are responsible for your own choices, actions and results.

This book is dedicated to my wife Diana,
and to our daughters, Megan and Mandy.
Each of them is a blessing for which I am endlessly grateful.

CONTENTS

INTRODUCTION

I am convinced that nothing we do is more important than hiring and developing people.
At the end of the day, you bet on people, not on strategies.

—Lawrence Bossidy,
former chairman and CEO of AlliedSignal

If you are involved in making hiring decisions, you need this book. It's practical, clear, and to the point. This book will help you see behind the candidate's mask to discover the real person who sits before you.

This is the first of three volumes. Volume 2 will deal with advanced assessment techniques, innovative assessment approaches, hiring for specific jobs, how to make the offer and get the new person started, executive types to be wary of, and a variety of other topics. Volume 3 will be a portfolio of observation forms, interview guides, and decision-making tools ready to be copied and put to use.

You'll find that many of the most common hiring problems are mentioned more the once. That's deliberate. The more often you see something, the more likely you will remember it.

This book is not designed to be a substitute for legal advice. Whenever you have questions about whether a procedure is within the law, I encourage you to consult a lawyer with specific expertise in this area.

HOW THIS BOOK CAME ABOUT

Over the last forty years, I have spent a major portion of my practice as a psychologist helping organizations make hiring decisions. At last count, I have been personally involved in more than three thousand decisions and many thousands more indirectly. In every case the challenge was to discover who this person really was.

This experience has led me to a several conclusions about hiring that seem to be valid worldwide.

SIX OBSERVATIONS ABOUT HIRING

1. Hiring the wrong person is one of the most expensive mistakes that organizations make. Many people have tried to estimate the cost of a hiring mistake. There are numerous formulas around. Each is calculated using different assumptions. As a best guess, in hiring for an entry-level position, the organization is risking a minimum of six times that person's annual salary. The more senior the role, the more expensive the dollar cost of a mistake.

2. Most (though not all) organizations do only a mediocre job of staff selection. There are several reasons for this. Very few staff assigned to hire people have had training in how to do so. Most people are involved on an intermittent basis, making it difficult to get any real skill. Often, there isn't enough time allowed to do the job properly. The pressure of "we have to get someone in that job" takes precedence over the appropriate caution. The decision maker then hires the mask, not the person.

3. The individual interview, particularly when done in an unstructured way, is notoriously unreliable in predicting job success. With this approach, even the best judge of character won't have the data needed to form a proper opinion. It has also become increasingly difficult to obtain really honest reference checks.

4. Hiring is subject to the law of supply and demand. In times of full employment, good people are hard to find. It's very likely that they already have a job. If they're good, their employer is doing everything possible to look after them. Often, the person you want to hire isn't even in the job market.

5. We never do someone a favor by hiring them into a job for which they are not suited.

> *A client wanted to hire a personal assistant to the managing director. Despite many danger signals suggesting that this candidate would be a poor choice, she was hired. Part of the client's reasoning was that "she looked the part and was pleasant. She may not be perfect, but she'll grow into the job."*
>
> *By the third week, it became clear that this hire had been a terrible mistake. Several weeks later, she was fired.*

Putting aside the cost to the organization, did they do this woman any favors? I think not.

6. Hiring involves evaluating human nature. This is a challenging exercise. At the interview, we see candidates at their very best. Some are skilled at putting on an acceptable and even persuasive interview mask. Once hired, the employee's personality will most certainly make itself known. Although it is possible to objectively assess credentials and to some extent confirm work experience, it is exceptionally difficult to really assess the candidate's personality before hiring.

You may be one of those people who believes you are a really good judge of others. This may well be true—in some circumstances. For example, if you know someone well, you have seen them in a variety of circumstances, and they are being entirely candid with you, then making judgments about that person's character won't be too difficult. The job interview is quite different.

EIGHT CHALLENGES TO JUDGING HUMAN NATURE IN A JOB INTERVIEW

1. You will have a relatively short period of time with the candidate.

2. The candidate's job is to highlight their strengths.

3. You are seeing the candidate in their very best light.

4. There is a strong incentive to downplay any weaknesses the candidate is aware of.

5. There may be other weaknesses the candidate is unaware of or may even regard as assets.

6. For the most part, you will have to rely on accepting what the candidate tells you about themselves.

7. Legal limits will prohibit you from asking some questions that you would like answered.

8. Most importantly, you are trying to predict how this person will act in the future, under circumstances that you can't always predict.

SOME OBVIOUS MISTAKES

Hiring the wrong person is an easy mistake to make. Let's look at some really catastrophic hiring errors.

Bankrupting the Bank

Founded in 1762 in London, Barings was the second oldest merchant bank in the world. They had a distinguished record. Among their historical achievements was facilitating the Louisiana Purchase, one of the most significant land sales in history. At the time this doubled the size of the United States. Barings also helped the United States finance the War of 1812 between the United States and the United Kingdom.

> **"Mr. Leeson was sentenced to six years in jail. Barings bank was declared bankrupt."**

In 1992 the bank decided to move into the Futures and Options business. Futures trading involves highly speculative bets on which way certain currencies will move. They hired Mr. Nick Leeson from

London to run both the front and back offices. At first, Mr. Leeson made several trades that were highly profitable for the bank. Soon, however, he began to fall deeply behind, despite providing glowing reports of his success to head office. By 1995, he had lost $1.4 billion. This was twice the amount of the bank's available trading capital.

Mr. Leeson was sentenced to six and half years in jail. Barings Bank was declared bankrupt and was sold for £1, about U.S. $2.00 today.

Killing Those You Care For

In 2011, a nursing home in the suburbs north of Sydney, Australia, needed a nurse to work the night shift. Not surprisingly, they had trouble finding someone. Nurses who want to work in aged care are notoriously difficult to attract, and finding those who want to work at night increased the difficulty.

Mr. Roger Dean approached an Aged Care provider, asking if they had work. They confirmed with relevant authorities that he did hold a practicing certificate as a nurse. His résumé showed that he had been employed in a coffee shop for the last four years. This didn't seem to attract the attention of anyone doing the hiring.

Soon after he started, his coworkers became convinced that he had a drug problem. The day came when he expected to be confronted by management (something about several hundred missing codeine tablets). The night before, he took two beds and set them on fire. This led to the immediate death of eleven residents. Several more died shortly afterward in the hospital. Mr. Dean was sentenced to life in prison.

HOW COULD IT GO THIS WRONG?

In both cases, dramatic clues had been overlooked.

Imagine you are hiring someone to work in Hong Kong, and the person's direct reporting relationship is to someone in London. You choose to hire someone who has a record of fraud. For the first few years, he sends you reports showing the wonderful profits he's made. Unfortunately, you have no way of independently verifying this.

This hiring mistake was made primarily because someone was blinded by this man's reputation of being a "shrewd trader". This rumored skill was given more weight than a proven history of fraud.

Hiring a nurse to work in an aged-care facility means literally giving someone the power to make life-and-death decisions. As it is not a glamorous industry, it can be difficult to find the right person. In this case, what efforts were made to attract a nurse are unknown.

What is known is that no one bothered to check Mr. Dean's past employment history. The fact that a nurse described himself as working in a coffee shop for the last four years seems not to have piqued anyone's interest.

These checks were made after he was arrested. They showed that in a prior job he had been investigated for workplace misconduct. He also had been sent home from work because it was suspected that he was under the influence of drugs. He also had been fired from a previous job because it was suspected that he damaged his supervisor's car.

> **Hiring someone is easy. Hiring the right person is extremely difficult.**

This mistake was caused by a combination of desperation and placing far too much weight on technical qualifications. There was little evidence of any attempt to understand the applicant's personality.

THE REALLY SAD PART

In the case of Mr. Leeson, the risk of problems was staring the bank personnel in the face. A history of fraud would be one of the first reasons to not hire someone to work in a bank.

This one hiring mistake led to the collapse of a two-hundred-year-old, highly respected institution. How many people lost their jobs? How did the senior executives explain to themselves, and to others, how this had happened?

In the case of Roger Dean, how does anyone explain this to the grieving relatives? Imagine being an old man or woman trapped in your bed in the middle of the night and burning to death, while in a place where you expect to be cared for.

WHAT CAN WE LEARN?

These decisions were made in the ordinary course of a business day. They looked like routine decisions to fill an empty job. The most important lesson from these two cases is to ask at the outset what the risks are to your organization if the wrong person is hired. Did anyone think of the risk that went with the hiring decision in these cases? Did "What if we get this wrong?" cross anyone's mind? I think not.

. . .

A SIMPLE SUMMARY

First and foremost, hiring is a risk management decision.

CHAPTER 1

LEADERSHIP AND HIRING

Management is doing things right; leadership is doing the right things.

—Peter Drucker, Management Consultant, known as The Father of Modern Management

Entering the word *leadership* into Google yields more hits than *the Beatles*. Even with that much in print, I'd like to add a few thoughts on leadership. I hope that my experience as a corporate psychologist can offer some new perspectives, with particular attention to the subject of hiring.

One thing stands out to me: To be a leader, you must know where you're going. Having the right staff will determine whether you get there.

THE FIRST JOB OF A LEADER

The role of a leader is to create a powerful, compelling vision. This can be an idea, a goal, or an image. It should be big and exciting. To be successful, it must be something that will motivate people and give them something to work toward. It must be unquestionably compelling. As one early employee of Apple said, *"Everybody wanted to work, not because we had to but because it was something we really believed in, something that was really going to make a difference."*

The purpose of a vision is to tell you, your staff, and your customers where exactly you intend to go. It states what you stand for. This can't be wishy-washy fluff, as is seen in too many "vision" posters hanging on office walls.

Google's vision is *"to organize the world's information and make it universally accessible and useful."* Would that get you out of bed in the morning? I bet it would.

Let's take a look at the more typical vision statement. This one comes from a corporate law firm: *"We strive to work with our clients toward our mutual success."* The idea of cold mashed potatoes springs to mind.

Think about where you work now. Is there a clear vision that really engages you? One to which everyone is committed? I mean really committed. Is it something that's worth getting out of bed for? Is it something you would happily share with all your customers? Something you would choose to be at least partially accountable for?

No, I didn't think so.

Most places have nothing resembling this. That's because it's hard to develop. And the more sharply you define your goals, the more things you have to say no to. Apple is quite open in stating, *"We believe in saying no to thousands of projects, so that we can really focus on the few that are truly important and meaningful to us."*

SAMPLE VISION STATEMENTS

Let's look at some well-known companies and their vision statements:

- **Tesla:** To accelerate the world's transition to sustainable energy

- **TED:** Spread ideas

- **Alzheimer's Association:** A world without Alzheimer's disease

- **Disney:** To make people happy

- **IKEA:** To create a better everyday life for people

- **Sony:** To be a company that inspires and fulfills your curiosity

All these are sharply worded, exciting, and they each create a picture of the future. Would any of these not excite you?

Creating a vision statement is something that budding entrepreneurs could do themselves. Many have begun in just that way. Pretty soon, though, more will be required.

WHAT DO YOU NEED NEXT?

You will need to attract and select the right people. They will be the engines that will help make your vision a reality. In a start-up business, the first ten people you hire will play a fundamental role in determining the success of that business. With such a small staff, even one person who doesn't fit will be like an anchor holding the ship from moving forward.

The single most important thing a leader can do is hire the right people. Nothing is more important. Nothing. Without the right people, translating your vision into reality will be a pretty tough slog.

Hiring staff is not for the fainthearted. (This is particularly true if you are a business owner. You will—literally—pay all the costs of hiring the wrong person.) It is a difficult task, leading you down a road filled with potential traps. If you've had any experience with selecting staff, the painful lessons learned are seared into your brain. You're determined to not fall into that trap again. (After all, that's why you bought this book, right?)

> **The single most important thing a leader can do is to hire the right people. Nothing is more important. Nothing!**

When assembling a new team or replacing those who have left, wise leaders will happily take complete responsibility for hiring. Experience has taught them that time and effort at the front end will pay handsome dividends when the best staff are selected.

Some readers will be working in big organizations. Hiring is delegated. "HR takes care of that" springs to mind. That may be how the organization chart reads. Taking this too literally can be like buying a ticket on the *Titanic*.

A decision as important as selecting someone to join your team cannot be left to others. There is too much at stake, and when things go sour, it's you who will bear the cost, not human resources.

THE IMPORTANCE OF PLANNING

Hiring is a very expensive exercise. The more senior the role, the greater the cost and the greater the risks. Experienced managers know this. They plan ahead, anticipating when staff will be needed. This allows everyone the time to do the job properly.

When an unexpected opening occurs, these managers know that it is almost always wiser to bring in temporary help. In essence, it's easier to end the relationship after one date than after being married for five years. Most importantly, the time, cost, and effort will all be seen as an investment rather than as an expense.

THE PROBLEM PERFORMER

What happens when a problem performer is allowed to join? The team's motivation will be compromised. The time spent managing the poor performer will add unnecessary stress for the leader. As motivation declines, the team becomes less efficient. Good people may leave, especially if the problem isn't dealt with promptly. This is just the start of the problems you'll have.

Not sure if this is right? Think about a time you worked with—or for—someone who was a clear hiring mistake. What effect did it have on you?

> **The first method for estimating the intelligence of a leader is to look at the people he has around them.**
> **- Machiavelli**

THE OPPORTUNITY COST

Often overlooked is this question: *"Where would we be if we had hired a competent person who did the job and who got along with us?"* (I'll give you a minute to think about this. Any more than a minute becomes too depressing.)

At a minimum, the organization would be moving toward its goals, not standing still or going backward. All the energy taken up with discipline, retraining, costly meetings with union members, termination payments, time replacing good staff who have left, and a host of other activities could be invested in making that vision a reality.

THE REWARDS OF DILIGENT HIRING

The right person will make your job as a leader much easier. Good people don't require being managed. They just get on with the job. Good people naturally set high standards for themselves. They get satisfaction from doing a job well. They'll be a consistent support to you. Yet some leaders can see hiring as a distraction from their "main job."

> *Newly hired staff working in aged care are expected to look after elderly, frail, and vulnerable people. Much of their work is done alone with residents. Often, it requires quite intimate contact. Employees who lack empathy, are overly aggressive, or are lazy will endanger residents' welfare.*

> *Our client employed a facility manager who would strive to finish interviews in about twenty minutes. When I*

discussed this with her, she said, "Look, I just don't have
the time for this. They're only entry-level staff. I'd spend
more time if this was a manager's position."

The manager was missing the point. These "entry-level staff" are the people closest to the residents. They are where the highest risk of inappropriate care is. When these staff make a mistake, the consequences can be extremely serious.

Among many other problems, this facility had a turnover of almost 40 percent among staff hired within the first year of service. (No wonder they did a lot of hiring.)

• • •

A SIMPLE SUMMARY

Getting the right person takes time and effort.
There are no shortcuts.

CHAPTER 2
. . . .

THE CHALLENGE OF HIRING

The gift of the badly adjusted is to charm you and make you want to hire them.

—John Wareham, founder and chairman
of Wareham Associates

Selecting the right person for a job is a very complex exercise, often more difficult than it may seem. The right choice will benefit everyone. Selecting an unsuitable person will cause untold difficulty, particularly if you will be supervising them.

One other thing: these mistakes are very expensive, much more so than most people realize.

How do you do it?

HOW TO BEGIN THE HIRING PROCESS

Begin by thinking about how much effort you want to put into the task.

As an example, consider a situation where a teenager, perhaps from a foreign country, is being chosen to live with you for six months. Once the student moves in on the first day, it will be difficult to change the plan. You've been told that "the school staff will choose the students and match them up with the host families." Somehow, this plan seems to be missing something.

How much screening would you want to do before exposing this person to your family on a daily basis? I can already hear the answer. A lot!

Let's suppose that you have a great team. Staff are loyal to you, to the company, and to one another. All are excellent at dealing with clients. They get along well, and each brings complementary skills.

You are hiring some-one new. Once hired, that person will live with your "work family" five days a week. How much screening do you want to do before ex-posing this person to a

> **The right employee can create a seismic shift in your company— start moving you faster (a lot faster), and grow in new ways.**
> **- Tony Robbins**

very valuable resource, one that has taken years to build up?

You want to be very careful about your choice. There are several obstacles to overcome. In this chapter, I'll outline some of the most common ones.

THE FIVE LACKS FOUND IN (ALMOST) EVERY HIRING PROCESS

1. Lack of a Structured Selection System to Follow

It's rare for a company to have a standardized approach to selecting staff. More commonly, each person (or each department) makes it up as they go along. No one is really sure of what questions worked better than others. As new people come and go, the approach can change dramatically. What served as a template for one round of recruitment can easily change for the next round. The practical experience of earlier staff is lost as new ones effectively start over.

A man applied to be a police officer. Preliminary background checking identified him as being a high-risk candidate. He was then ruled out for further consideration.

In the coming months, there were several personnel changes in the recruitment section. New staff hadn't been trained on how to use the interview system and were also unaware of the earlier selection result.

At the next recruitment campaign, this unsuccessful applicant applied again. This time, the applicant "modified" the background checks. As this was the second time he was given the same interview, he remembered some of the questions. This allowed for offering "improved" responses. This previously high-risk candidate was then hired.

Performance problems appeared during training and at his first job assignment. He was described as arrogant, difficult to supervise, and reluctant to follow procedures. These problems persisted for several years until he ultimately resigned.

A structured system is designed to protect you from this type of mistake. It means knowing in advance what step comes first and then what comes next—all the way through to making the final decision. Criteria are established for deciding when applicants should be advanced in the process or when they are considered unsuitable.

The interview questions are all carefully thought out. They are tailored for the particular vacancy to be filled. All applicants—and I mean *all*—are expected to complete each step of the process.

The best staff are kept involved in hiring for at least several years. Appropriate training is provided at the outset. Strict criteria are set for what a new team member must do before being allowed to interview applicants.

Most importantly, all this is documented so that someone new can pick it up quickly.

2. Lack of Techniques to Probe Beneath the Surface

The candidates are there to get the job. They are expected to sell themselves. They will emphasize their strengths and will be reluctant to reveal any past problems.

Questions like "Tell me about your weaknesses" or "Describe a difficult problem you successfully solved at work" are very unlikely to yield useful information. A glance at Amazon books will show you the extensive manuals available to help applicants answer the toughest interview questions. (In Volume 2 I'll describe how to deal with the person who has rehearsed answers.)

On the other hand, some questions are very likely to give you information that would other wise be unavailable. For example, "Suppose you could instantly change anything about your personality, not counting your height, weight, or eye color. What would you change?" This is a question that applicants are very unlikely to have prepared for. The response given is therefore much more likely to be revealing.

This question is harder to prepare for. The answer will give you a look inside the mask.

What else will work? I'll show you that in the upcoming chapters. To be appreciated here is that the "standard" approaches to an interview are often remarkably limited.

3. Lack of Training

There is a belief that once someone is promoted to a leadership role, they automatically know how to select staff. This is obviously not true.

Choosing who to hire is both a technical skill and an art. Much of it can be learned with appropriate training. In reality, most peo- ple learn on the job. This means that they are improvising most of the time. Often their teachers don't know very much about hiring, because they have been muddling along for years. This is a very inefficient (and expensive) way to learn. (I sure hope that someone counts the cost of their hiring mistakes, but I'm not optimistic.)

An experienced public servant, moving to another agency, was appointed to oversee recruiting entry-level staff. His past experience in human resources was limited to working on payroll. He arrived anxious to prove that he knew what he was doing. In his second week, he was advised that a group of five applicants were not being advanced.

He decided that it would be best if he interviewed them. After a twenty-minute informal chat with each candidate, he decided that each was suitable. Subordinates, all of whom had more experience in hiring, and who completed formal training in hiring, tried to explain that this wasn't a good idea. He would have none of it. After all, he was "an experienced HR professional, and I knew how to pick good people."

Two years after being hired, all five were chronic and serious problem performers to the agency. Meanwhile, the person who hired them had moved to another agency about six months after these staff members started work.

4. Lack of Practice

We get better at things with practice. Think of how hard it was to drive when you were learning. After lots of practice, it became automatic. This is true for most skills we learn.

Learning to hire staff is the same, but for most people, practice comes only intermittently. Think how often you are called on to make a hiring decision. It's difficult to develop real skill when only practicing occasionally.

The next critical element of learning a skill is getting feedback on how accurate you are. Imagine learning to hit a golf ball. Would you want to know where each practice shot landed? Sure you would. Now imagine hiring staff and never having a really clear idea of who was a good choice and who wasn't.

> **An ounce of practice is worth more than tons of preaching.**
> **- Mahatma Gandhi**

5. Lack of Time

People assigned to hire someone will commonly report that they don't have enough time. What naturally happens is that interviews get squeezed into an already busy day, and there is a strong push to "hurry up."

The job application materials can be given a cursory glance rather than a careful study. Interview questions get made up on the spot, or an old "standard" interview form gets pulled out.

Under these conditions, hiring someone can seem like just another task on the to-do list. The effect of making the wrong decision is overlooked. Things might change when a problem performer is invited to join the team, but even this isn't enough to rigorously review the system.

These five "lacks" are universal. Whether you work in a large multinational or a firm of five staff, you can expect to encounter at least one—and usually more. You may need to change the mind of the decision maker about how that person wants selection to be done. If you are the decision maker, I'd suggest reading this chap- ter again until you have it memorized.

Yes, it really is that important.

· · ·

A SIMPLE SUMMARY

Obstacles will always be there. The time to develop solutions is not when you are recruiting but when you aren't.

CHAPTER 3

FIRST DECIDE WHAT YOU NEED

Really good people are often harder to find than people with really good skills.

—Dr. Ken Byrne, Corporate Psychologist

B efore deciding who you want, first think about what you want the job to accomplish. Think about it as if the job had a life of its own, without any one person in it. A bit of straightforward, clear thinking goes a long way in assessing a job. The following ten questions will help.

TEN JOB ASSESSMENT QUESTIONS

1. What is the purpose of this job?

2. Is there someone I know who has done this job successfully?

3. What bad thing would happen if this job didn't exist?

4. What technical skill is absolutely required on day one?

5. What technical knowledge is required for adequate performance over the first six months?

6. What problems will the person in this job be expected to solve independently, and at what point will guidance of a more senior role be required?

7. How much freedom will the person in this job have to make decisions?

8. Who will the person in this job have to interact with?

9. Who—if anyone—will the person in this job have to persuade or influence?

10. What are the interpersonal dynamics of the group the person will work with?

Now that you've got a rough idea of what you need, here's what to do next.

FIVE STEPS FOR PUTTING JOB ASSESSMENT INTO PRACTICAL TERMS

Step 1: Write a one-page summary to describe the job.
The following are seven sentence starters to formulate a job summary:

1. The purpose of this job is to...

2. The results the person in this job will be accountable for are...

3. The person in this job will interact with...

4. The person in this job is expected to persuade these people through direct authority...

5. The person in this job is expected to persuade these people without direct authority...

6. The person in this job will be expected to solve problems like...

7. The biggest challenges of this job will be...

Try writing this as if you were explaining to a friend what the job is all about.

Step 2: Define the skills that are essential to have on day one of employment.
This might include having a nursing degree, possessing a driver's license, or being credentialed in youth work. Ask whether it is possible for a candidate to start on day one without this skill or credential. If the answer is no, then it is an essential skill.

Step 3: List the essential personality traits.
Be realistic. Avoid the trap of wanting everything in one person. There are very few people who are "creative, big-picture thinkers"

and who are also "strong on detailed follow-through." Sounds funny, right? You have no idea how many times I've seen exactly this type of logic in job descriptions. Think about some of your ideal performers. What are the inherent personality traits that make each person so valuable?

The following are ten qualities to consider for almost every job summary:

1. Perseverance

2. Adequate intelligence

3. Practical judgment and common sense

4. Empathy toward others

5. Willingness to go the extra mile

6. Ability to read interpersonal situations

7. Readiness to accept responsibility for mistakes

8. Capacity to work cooperatively with others

9. Willingness to follow job guidelines

10. Humility

Step 4: List the skills that would be preferable for someone to have.

Remember that with the exception of essential skills, employees can be taught what they need to know. Consider how flexible you can be if someone comes along who meets your other criteria.

> **People get hired because of what they know. They are invariably fired because of who they are.**

I wanted to hire someone for our firm. Among the desirable skills was a minimum typing speed of sixty words per minute. We interviewed many people. Finally, I met someone who could type only twenty-two words per minute but who seemed to be exactly the type of person we wanted. I knew we could help her to learn to type faster. What we couldn't teach was a good work ethic, strong attention to client needs, sensitivity to others, and a host of other personal qualities that she had in abundance.

Understandably, it took her a bit longer to come to grips with the typing demands. This was a minor inconvenience. All her personal attributes helped her to quickly become successful and eventually be promoted. She is still a very valuable team member.

Step 5: Assess the value of experience.

Consider the kind of experience you would like someone to have. Try not to be too rigid in your thinking here. That's because experience does not always equal success. When hiring, especially when there is a shortage of applicants, experience can be given far too much weight.

A local church was looking for a youth leader. Of the two applicants, one stood out, primarily because he had held a similar job with another church in another state. Having just moved to a new state, his reason for being unemployed was obvious.

He made a very favorable impression during his only interview. The interview focused heavily on knowledge about youth work, an area in which he shined.

This candidate was hired and proved to be an endless headache to the pastor. He had trouble reading others, tended to be authoritarian, and irritated coworkers.

There is an underlying assumption that the business demand of one organization will be very similar to another. Although this is occasionally true, much more often, it turns out not to be. This is because each business is guided by its own implied set of values. These define what behavior is accepted, what is frowned on, and what will attract some supervisory attention. These values are

> **Even two companies selling the same product will have quite different values. Successful performance in one company is certainly no guarantee of success in the other.**

usually unspoken and will often be quite different from what you read on the wall.

. . .

A SIMPLE SUMMARY

It is critical to first define what the job requires. Without a road map, it will be hard to find the destination.

CHAPTER 4

CREATE A COMPELLING ATTRACTION STRATEGY

You can't hire the best people unless you're meeting the best.
—Lou Adler, founder of the Adler Group

H iring is a lot like fishing. You are looking to attract the largest and most beautiful fish available. You need bait, something that will let the fish know there is something attractive to pursue.

FISHING IN THE RIGHT POND

A recently graduated HR consultant was hired. Part of her job was to find suitable candidates for entry-level blue collar traineeships.

She thought that a good place to look would be in the pool of long-term unemployed people who were part of a government scheme to help them find work.

This was unsuccessful. None of the original pool of about eighteen applicants was even close to being ready for work.

The recruitment manager didn't give enough thought to some of the basic requirements of this entry-level job. For example, people were expected to report to work on time, to follow basic safety procedures, to have basic literacy and numeracy skills, and to demonstrate a keenness to learn.

People from this group of applicants had been so disadvantaged by life, and had taken enough knocks to their self-confidence, that these expectations were beyond them. Could someone from this pool have been successful? Perhaps. But is this where you would want to invest scarce resources to find applicants? I think not.

WHAT'S ATTRACTIVE ABOUT YOU

You must be able to answer this question, which will be in the mind of potential applicants: *"Why should I work for you?"*

What are the psychological rewards that working for you can offer? (If you can't think of any, you've got a lot of work to do.) Be creative in looking for what distinguishes you from others recruiting in the same pool.

> *A small accounting firm wanted to attract new graduates. The big firms invariably snapped up the best people. They determined that by having staff work slightly longer days, everyone could have one day off work every two weeks. That's something the big guys could never offer. They've never had difficulty attracting a good pool of new graduates since.*

You must be able to say, with your hand on your heart, why your organization would be a good place to work. High salaries? Not enough. A big salary is a good way to get people to move jobs. It's a terrible way to keep people.

You must be able to find the psychological rewards that someone can reasonably expect to experience working for you.

> **You must be able to say, hand on heart, why your organization would be a good place to work.**

TEN COMMON PSYCHOLOGICAL REWARDS PEOPLE EXPECT FROM THEIR JOBS

These are some of the more important psychological rewards that people look for. Some people will also have unique rewards that are important to them. In volume 2, I'll show you how to elicit these unique values. The more of these that a job can offer, the more likely it is that you will have a range of quality candidates.

1. Feeling that my opinion matters

2. Enjoying the people I work with

3. Receiving appreciation or acknowledgement for work I have done

4. Job security

5. Pride in the product or service that our company offers

6. Located close to home

7. Working hours are flexible, with some capacity to adjust them to my schedule

8. Feeling loyalty and support from my supervisor

9. The opportunity to learn new skills

10. The chance to feel a sense of achievement

How many of these can your company meet on a regular basis?

THE DANGER OF HAVING ONLY ONE CANDIDATE

You aren't looking for just anyone who will take the job. You want to attract several suitable applicants, all of whom meet most of the criteria you specified in your job summary. You never—ever—want to have just one candidate.

> *A firm advertised several times in the newspaper for a book-keeper. Only one vaguely suitable person answered the ads. That applicant was hired not because he was particularly strong but out of desperation. That new employee quickly became a marginal performer.*

The lessons are clear. Don't hire out of desperation. Never rely on just one method to recruit people.

THE SECRET TO ATTRACTING
THE BEST APPLICANTS

Create a compelling culture. That's it. Four words. Motivated, enthusiastic employees are your best recruiting tool. They're the ones who others want to emulate. What better way to do that than by joining their company?

You may think that only people at the top can shape company culture. That's only partly true. You can absolutely play a role in shaping the culture where you work.

> *A young law graduate joined a large commercial firm. She quickly learned that professional staff worked eighty-hour weeks. Five years later, she is still there and thriving. Why? The company culture. She said, "We do really good work. I'm surrounded by talented people who are fun to work with. I learn a lot from the more senior people."*

The partners she works for are fair-minded and generous. She feels that they have her best interests at heart. Although she was told about her mistakes, this was invariably done in a constructive manner. When asked about working in other areas of the firm, she commented, "*Not on your life!*"

Ask yourself why you work where you do. What is it that keeps you there? Make a list of these things. Do you use this when telling people about the job opening you have? You should.

One suggestion: if you can't think of any reason why someone would want to work at your place, you're probably not the best person to be involved with recruitment.

TWELVE HIGH-VALUE STRATEGIES FOR ATTRACTING CANDIDATES

1. Look in-house. As part of your search strategy, start with people in the business who could be promoted. It may be that the perfect person doesn't work for you, but a very strong person might. Sometimes this may require more training time than would ideal. This has to be traded against the risk of bringing in someone new.

2. Create a recruitment video. If you're younger than fifty, feel free to skip this paragraph. For you older folks (and you know who you are), here's a news flash. People no longer get information mainly by reading. Younger people want to learn things by watch-ing videos. If you're trying to get people's attention, it's a good idea to put that message in a package that will best do that. Get a group of enthusiastic staff (preferably under age thirty) who have smartphones (as if anyone in that group wouldn't have one!). Have a look at videos done by other companies. Be sure to examine those you are competing with for applicants.

Keep it under three minutes. Give the team very broad directives, making sure they know this is for the purpose of attracting new applicants. Now get out of their way.

3. Create a recruitment culture. This means that everyone in the organization, from the top down, sees it as part of their job to be on the lookout for good people. This is true even if you're not hiring at the moment.

In the course of doing business you – and each of your staff - will inevitably come across people who you'd like to have working with you. If you're feeling particularly bold, tell them there is on opportunity with your company. Ask if they'd like to know more about it. If they say "Yes" you my have a candidate. If they say "No", this allows you to make the following offer:

> *"I can certainly understand if this isn't right for you now. Let me tell you about a policy we have. Whenever we meet someone who we think would be a great fit for our business, we ask their permission to be on our Platinum Candidate's List. That way, if something comes up that we think might interest you in future, we can be in touch. Of course, we only do that with the permission of the other person. Would you mind if I added you name to the list?"*

> *Very few people will say no. Then you can exchange business cards and continue your conversation. Of course, if they hear about the job and turn you down, you can still add them to the Platinum list for when something else comes up.*

> *Someone should be designated as The Keeper of the Platinum List. When you have an opening, and you're satisfied there are no suitable internal applicants, this should be the next stop for you.*

There are two cautions to be alert to using this strategy:

- Only make the offer to a person you think could be a stand out candidate. Offer this too often and it cheapens it. It also makes you look desperate.

- When you tap the Platinum List, or when someone you know and trust recommends an applicant, there is a temptation to shortcut the usual screening process. Make it clear to everyone—yourself included—that anyone who is referred must go through the same selection process as everyone else.

4. Use Your Company Website. Create a tab that says "Like to Work With Us?". Make sure it is easy to find. You can list as many or as few of the jobs you are hiring for. Make sure you describe the job in a way that the reader will easily understand.

> *One of our clients wanted to hire people with a security background. Part of their business was managing a series of low cost housing units. They needed people to do a casual patrol, being available to negotiate disputes, help out with very minor repairs and to ensure that the correct number of people were living there. How was the job described in their advertising? "Administration Officer wanted."*

Put the video we described above on the website. It should be located "front and center". Right next to it should be a phone number to call for more information. Make absolutely certain that the person who answers that phone (and anyone who fills in for them) has a warm, welcoming voice and is able to describe the job in positive terms.

5. Ask Your Best Employees for a Testimonial
Explain that you'd like a short testimonial describing what it's like to work at your company. Post these next to the "Like to Work With Us" tab on your website. People want to know what it's really like

working for you. Your best employees are the ones to tell them. If you don't have anyone who qualifies as a "best employee" be sure to read Volume 2 where I talk about company culture.

6. Follow previous good performers. Keep track of good performers who have left. People can leave your organization for a variety of reasons. Maybe they had a conflict with someone who no longer works there. Perhaps they disagreed with a policy that has been changed. Whatever the reason for leaving, it's always a good idea to contact prior employees who you know are suitable. (If you are turned down, you could ask if they know anyone who might be the right fit. After all, they know your business and the type of people who do well there.)

7. Remember Your Old Friends. Make it known to your friends and associates that you want to fill a particular job. Give them enough information to allow them to scan their lists of contacts to see if they know anyone who would be suitable.

> *A client was looking to hire a third-year lawyer. Two partners in charge of the project had advertised extensively and used two search firms, all without success. (Third-year lawyers who are any good are well looked after.) I asked each of them to make a list of everyone they knew who might know of someone. My reasoning was that someone they know might know someone who would be interested. They sent emails to more than one hundred people. In two weeks, they had three strong applicants. After completing the selection process, one was hired.*

8. Make new friends. Whoever it is you want to recruit, and no matter how specialized the role, there are people who know the people you want to meet.

A general practitioner running a highly specialized practice was at a loss to find doctors who shared the same values as she and her team. She had been paying a recruitment agency an outrageous sum to locate a general practitioner. If this person were hired, there was absolutely no guarantee for the fee that was paid. If they left the next day, well, too bad.

With some discussion, several opportunities were identified:

- *In any given city, there are programs that certify doctors as being ready for general practice. Our friend had not even considered meeting those people. Yet they could be the ideal people to spot the kind of talent she was looking for.*

- *One of the doctors who worked there, and who was an excellent performer, joined the practice after migrating from overseas. When considering the fee being paid to an agency, this could easily be used to support several trips to other countries, searching for people who shared the same values as our doctor friend.*

- *There are usually more applicants for specialist training positions than there are jobs available. This leaves a group of medical graduates who are unable to be specialists. Many of them do additional training to become*

a general practitioner. Our friend needed to meet the
people who run those programs.

9. Develop relationships with training facilities. Many training institutes employ someone whose job is to look for employment for graduates. Contact this person and let them know in advance about the kind of roles you have open and the kind of people you're looking for. Stay in touch and give feedback on people they have referred.

10. Create your own training program. Many schools require students to gain practical, real-world experience. Consider developing an internship program. Students who are not yet ready for employment might be suitable as interns. Usually this requires you to provide some teaching in return for free or low-cost labor. This is an excellent way to have a preliminary look at potential employees.

A variation is to recruit final-year students who want to work during their summer holidays. This gives you a chance to get to know potential permanent employees and to develop company loyalty. Few people are as grateful as ambitious university students given a chance to do real work, and to gain practical experience, while earning a few dollars over the school holidays.

An aged care facility created internship programs for nursing, social work, and psychology students. (From the school's point of view, there are never enough of these placements.)

They had great success. Surprisingly, some of the students who would have never considered a career in aged care looked much more favorably on it. Some went on to join the organization when they completed training.

A key factor in whether this will work is the quality of people whom students are assigned to work with and the talent of whoever is supervising them.

> **Whoever it is you want to recruit, and no matter how specialised the role, there are people who know the people you want to meet. Go meet them.**

11. Locate companies that are retrenching staff. You'll find many loyal, hardworking people with maturity and life experience on their side. They're also about to be unemployed. You know they will be looking for work. But they might not consider working in your industry unless you tell them what's available.

When you hear of a company that's retrenching people, contact them immediately. Let them know the kind of people you're looking for. Make it clear that you're willing to train capable applicants. (I assure you, the company will be delighted to hear from you.)

12. Use university recruiting. Some firms actively recruit students graduating from university. This provides a chance to sell your organization as well as to employ younger people who can be trained over time to grow with the company.

FOUR LOWER-QUALITY THOUGH NECESSARY ATTRACTION STRATEGIES

1. Newspaper advertising. Your ad must quickly get the reader's attention and sell the positives of why that person should consider working for you. This requires a lot more thought than saying, "We have a job, here's what you must have, and send in your application."

In volume 2, we'll look at this in more detail. For the moment, every ad you write must first answer these three questions:

- Why should I continue reading this ad?

- Why should I work for you rather than for someone else?

- What are the psychological rewards I can expect?

2. Internet advertising. The same rules apply to using social media or the Internet The challenge is to make the ad specific enough to tap your target audience yet not so broad that you get hundreds of inappropriate applications.

3. Personnel agencies. The major advantage of personnel agencies is that they can save you time. (The major disadvantage is that they can waste your time.) You must decide whether their service is worth their fee. Do not be lulled into a false sense of security. Usually, statements like "The agency is taking care of that" reveal this.

You must make the hiring decision. Remember that the consultant does not have the same objectives that you do. The less time they spend on the assignment, the greater their profit margin.

You must rigorously apply your selection process, even if the consultant thinks they have "*just the right person.*" Be aware that some time will have passed to allow the personnel consultant (who, after all, is the "expert" at this) to give you a short list. This can create an artificial sense of urgency on your part.

4. Search firms. Search firms are often necessary for particular jobs, typically higher-level management jobs and certain technical

or highly specialized positions. Good search firms can often un-
cover suitable people who may not be actively looking for a job
change.

Their results will be only as good as the consultant who is doing the search. Although someone with gray hair and a sparkling
white shirt will almost certainly land the assignment, sometimes it is
a junior consultant who does the actual work. You need to ask
what *specific* experience this person has had in finding applicants
in your business area.

The same caution about your expectations building up while
you wait are even more important here.

. . .

A SIMPLE SUMMARY

*Attracting the best fish requires looking in the right pond and ensuring
that you have the very best bait. Make sure the fish can see what's on offer.*

CHAPTER 5

· · · · · · · · · · · · · · ·

DESIGNING A FOOLPROOF SELECTION PROCESS

Hiring the right people takes time, the right questions and a healthy dose of curiosity. What do you think is the most important factor when building your team? For us, it's personality.

—Richard Branson, business magnate, author, and philanthropist

A selection process describes a series of steps that each applicant is required to complete before a selection decision is made. Sounds simple. Unfortunately, in all the companies where I've been a consulant, this either does not exist or is used intermittently by the various departments as it suits them.

Before going further, a brief confession is required. We all know that there is no such thing as a foolproof selection system. I used that title only because the publisher assured me it would help sell more books. On the other hand, if you use the tools in this book, you'll be getting closer to an ideal selection process than any of your competitors.

WHY YOU NEED A STRUCTURED APPROACH

A structured system that everyone must follow is a key part of your risk management strategy. (Hiring staff is one of the biggest risks one takes.) This will ensure that everyone involved with hiring will do things in (approximately) the same way. It also gives some confidence that the selection process will be as fair as possible and resistant to unreasonable legal challenge.

Some people will persist with the belief that hiring new staff is a distraction from their real jobs. This will lead to overlooking the amount of risk associated with the hiring decision. Having an agreed process that everyone is required to complete is your way of ensuring that no shortcuts are taken.

THE CHALLENGE OF A STRUCTURED SELECTION SYSTEM

This is not an easy process to develop or maintain. A great deal of preparation is necessary. Try to get support from the highest person in your company. Getting buy-in from those who will use this is also critically important. There will be resistance from some who believe that they are a good judge of people. Although that may be true, choosing appropriate staff requires much more than that.

FORMULATING A SELECTION PROCESS: WHAT DOESN'T WORK

There is enough myth surrounding hiring that assumptions can easily become facts. One person tells a friend about a clever trick they invented. It seemed to work (at least, as best as anyone can figure). By the time the friend tells someone else, this idea becomes a fact, proven beyond a doubt. Here are some techniques that have no basis in reality.

> **Brain teaser questions do nothing to help predict performance. They are almost certainly a waste of time.**

Trick Questions

A common approach to hiring uses brainteaser questions. For example:

- What song best describes your personality?

- How many golf balls will fit inside a 747?

- What do you think about when driving in your car?

These add nothing to predicting job performance and are a waste of time. They are almost certainly illegal.

The Unstructured Interview

Perhaps most common is when the interviewer makes up questions on the fly. Some may be quality questions. Others will be poor, and the risk of leading questions is very high.

> *One of our workshop trainers was in a coffee shop and re-ported overhearing the two people sitting next to him. It soon became clear that this was a job interview.*

> *The interviewer made up questions as they occurred to her. There seemed no discernible structure or logic to how questions were presented. One that stood out in our trainer's mind was this: "This job will require you to work with people from all levels of society. With your background, I guess you wouldn't have any trouble with this, would you?"*

What are the chances that the applicant said, *"Yes, now that I think about it, that would be particularly challenging for me"*?

There is considerable research on using the unstructured interview. Studies consistently show little correlation between interview rating and job performance.

Reference Checking Left to Junior Staff

Reference checking requires a great deal of skill to do well. It is an intricate dance, with one side wanting to find out what the candidate is really like. The other side (mostly) doesn't want to be the reason someone isn't hired.

Most applicants will put forth people who they know will say only positives about them and who will rarely say anything negative. A superficial reference check accomplishes just that and nothing more.

FORMULATING A SELECTION PROCESS:
WHAT DOES WORK

A Work Sample

Requesting a work sample means giving the candidate a sample piece of work, similar to what they will do in the job, and objectively assessing how well they perform.

> *A consulting firm used a variety of interviews and reference checks to select a new executive assistant for a senior partner. The last step was a typing test. The best candidate, who everyone was keen on, said that she typed about sixty-five to seventy words per minute. When tested, she typed fourteen words per minute, even with several tests. The firm decided to put the typing test earlier in their process.*

The following are several other work samples that can be used:

- **Accounting:** Give a profit and loss statement that you know has a certain number of errors contained within it. The applicant is asked to do the following: "Analyze this P and L and give us your recommendations."

- **Marketing:** Ask the person to provide a written critique of one section of your marketing plan. (If this is confidential, use a made-up one.) Ask them to summarize their opinions under two headings, "Facts" and "Opinions."

- **Management:** Create a new policy. It can be a real change or something developed for this exercise. Explain to the

> **The Work Sample and Audition Technique are among the two most powerful methods for helping to see the real person hiding behind the "interview mask"**

applicant what has prompted the thinking behind this new policy. It could be something to do with managing sick leave, how holiday time is accrued, controlling expenses related to sales, or some other topic. Ask each candidate to prepare a memo to the CEO. They should consider the advantages of this policy, the potential disadvantages, and conclude with a specific recommendation. Do not give any guidance about how long the memo should be.

The Audition Technique

This requires applicants to demonstrate the skills that they say they have. The title comes from the way people apply for a part in a play. How does the director decide who will be the best actor? Ask the candidates to demonstrate their ability to act. (Can you imagine making the decision based on what people claim they can do?)

The following are some examples of how the audition technique can be used in job selection:

- Ask an executive applicant to hold a meeting with a major customer who is unhappy.

- Ask a supervisory applicant to meet with an underperforming employee.

- Ask a sales applicant to meet with a major prospect who has just recently introduced several reasons for not buying.

- Ask a social worker applicant to meet with a challenging client.

- Ask a teacher applicant to counsel an underperforming student.

In each case, someone from the hiring panel will play the role of the client, staff member, employee or student. Create a short brief about the situation. Then the staff member responds spontaneously to each candidate's approach.

This need only run for three to five minutes. Do not mention the phrase *role-playing*. If the candidate asks, simply say, *"We'd just like to see how you approach this."* (It is only your team who is role-playing. The candidates are demonstrating their level of skill.)

A Test of Cognitive Ability
These are tests with right-or-wrong answers, similar to what would be found on an IQ test. People with higher scores will learn new information more quickly than those with lower scores. Volume 2 provides more information on this topic.

A Test Measuring Conscientiousness
This can give you a measure of how likely the candidate will persist with jobs to completion. This trait is quite variable among people, regardless of past experiences or self reports of being strong in this area.

The Unsung Genius of the Structured Interview
Structured interviews ask candidates a consistent set of questions with clear criteria to assess the quality of responses. Each question

will have a description of what would distinguish an average from an above-average answer. Here's an example:

Question: When working closely with other people, it's impossible to avoid conflict. Can you tell me about a time that you had conflict with someone at work?" (Follow-up question: "How did you deal with this?")

Average answer: The candidate is able to describe a conflict situation, indicates that they could read another person reasonably accurately, provides a basic solution, indicates only a modest effort to consider the needs of the other person, and doesn't describe any follow-up.

Above-average answer: The candidate provides a more complex problem that requires a more in-depth reading of another person, is able to clearly describe their understanding of the situation, provides an in-depth description of the outcome, and describes a deliberate effort to follow up to be sure that the situation is resolved.

Developing these questions, including scoring criteria, takes a good deal of time and thought. (More time! I bought this book because I thought it would help me save time!)

Where do you want to put in the time? Before hiring? Or would you prefer to put in a great deal more time and money managing a bad hiring decision?

THE POWER OF COMBINING TOOLS

So far, we've looked only at individual tools. What will work best is a combination of selection methods. These might include tests of learning ability and conscientiousness in addition to a variety of interviews and careful reference checking.

Keep in mind that a test, as long as it is a reasonable sample of the work the job requires, will give you a score. This is as close to a fact as you will find in recruitment. These should be given at least equal weight to impressionistic criteria from the interview, and sometimes more, in making a selection decision.

A financial services firm wanted to hire a client services manager. After interviewing people on their short list, they decided on one applicant and asked me to evaluate her against the requirements of the position. The new employee would have to do a considerable amount of reading, especially if the person was new to this industry. She would need strong mathematical skills. Diplomacy, self-control, and a reasonable level of persuasiveness were all important.

The applicant made a very positive impression on me. She possessed considerable charm, was enthusiastic about the job, and had a strong level of personal drive and self-confidence. However, in the interview, I also picked up a slight sense of arrogance and the potential for feeling better than others.

She scored 102 on a standard IQ test we use. (About 66 percent of people will score between 90 and 110.) Her reading score placed at the twenty-eighth percentile when compared to a group of midlevel managers. Her numerical reasoning skills were at the thirty-second percentile.

These scores meant that it would take her significantly longer to learn new information, and she would take much longer than expected to understand and retain information from reading; her ability to deal with numerical problems was also very low.

The client was unhappy to hear these results and wanted to persuade me that her strong interpersonal skills could be enough to overcome these findings. With further discussion, he mentioned that two of the people who interviewed her said that they picked up just a bit of a feeling that she would be hard to give feedback to (another sign of arrogance). This was dismissed in the group discussion as unimportant.

The client was very keen to hire this person and did so, even after being alerted to these potential problems. She was dismissed after about ten months of coaching, including trying to modify the job and sending her to reading improvement classes. With some probing, the client told me that she had alienated some of her peers, as she conveyed a sense "that she was better than the others."

I was unhappy for the client, knowing the cost of starting over. On the other hand, this type of case isn't bad for business.

In addition to combining tools, it is also important to conduct a thorough, skillful reference check from at least two of the candidate's prior bosses, not friends or colleagues.

. . .

A SIMPLE SUMMARY

Accomplishing anything requires using the best available tools. If you want mediocre results, then stick with ordinary tools.

CHAPTER 6

· · · · · · · · · · · · · · ·

BASIC INTERVIEW CONCEPTS

In looking for people to hire, you look for three things: integrity, intelligence, and energy. If you don't have the first, the other two will kill you.
—**Warren Buffett, legendary investment genius**

WHO SHOULD BE ON THE INTERVIEW PANEL

· ·

Who should be involved with the selection process and make up the interview selection panel? It should always be a group of people, but who should be included?

This will partly depend on the seniority of the role. Let's take two examples: an entry-level administrative assistant and a middle-level manager.

Administrative assistant applicant: Applicants who pass the initial screening steps should be interviewed by the person who will be their manager and by a group of peers.

Middle manager, operations: This person should be interviewed by a senior executive, by the person they will report to, by a group of peers, and by a group of staff who will report to them. Ideally, someone from outside this work area, say someone from legal or accounting, should also be involved.

This will require at least two visits to your office and perhaps more for the senior person. Take the time you need to formulate a thoughtful, evidence-based decision. Don't let yourself be rushed.

Every interview requires an exchange of information between two or more people. The principles discussed here are relevant to all interviews. They are particularly relevant when assessing a job candidate. Regardless of your hiring decision, you want that person to be telling their friends and family about the very thoughtful and professional approach you used.

THE BEST VENUE

The best venue is usually your own office or a conference room. Do not to take phone calls or permit other interruptions while the interview is in progress. Proper interviewing requires uninterrupt- ed time and plenty of concentration. Throughout the interview, give the candidate your undivided attention. (If this is a challenge, just remember how much money is riding on this decision.)

Avoid having a desk between you and the candidate. An imposing desk tends to set up a wall. Bring your chair around to the front of the table. This conveys your interest in talking openly.

SIX KEY PRINCIPLES FOR CONDUCTING
AN EFFECTIVE INTERVIEW

These six principles are critically important to your success in recruiting the right person. Violating any of these, even in what appears to be a small way, will jeopardize your success.

1. Always be considerate to the candidate. Remember that you are selling yourself and your company. The candidate will undoubtedly tell other people about their experience with you. Good news travels fast, and bad news travels even faster. Google achieved the outcome you want. They use an extensive, time-consuming selection process. They found that 80 percent of people who had been turned down for a job would still recommend Google as an employer.

> **All good interviewers have one thing in common. Without exception they are good listeners.**

The people you turn down can be an adjunct to your attraction strategy. They can also talk down you and your company, potentially discouraging good people from applying.

2. Develop rapport. The first task of the interview is to develop rapport. This means that you want to understand the candidate's feelings or ideas and to let them know yours. You want to create a feeling that each of you understands the goal of the interview.

The ground rules for establishing rapport are friendliness and honesty. You must have a genuine interest in the candidate. Even though for you they may be the fifth person you have seen for the job, for the candidate, this is a very important meeting, one that may change the course of their life.

The candidate will be nervous and will have questions. The way in which you open the interview should deal with both of these factors. You might begin by explaining where you fit in the organization and what your role is regarding the hiring process.

Explain that you want to use the time that's available to get to know the candidate. Any questions should be dealt with in a straightforward way.

3. Do not ask any questions that could be seen as reflecting discrimination. Questions that ask about religion, gender, race, color, national origin, sexual orientation, pregnancy, disability, age, marital status, number of children, or citizenship are illegal. They should never be asked directly. We'll look at how to ask some of these indirectly in volume 2.

Note that I have phrased this as "could be seen as." Discrimination can be seen in any question or comment. The best you can do is to have a written record of the questions asked and the responses given. This seems pretty obvious, right? It's not to everyone.

> Our client was trying to fill a very senior, technical role. There were perhaps twenty people in the country who could be considered. After a ten-month professional search, a strong candidate was identified.
>
> A senior executive who reported to the CEO conducted the first interview. Early in the interview, he asked about this woman's past work experiences. This included the reasons for leaving each of her most recent jobs. To explain one job change, she said, "I was going through a divorce, and my

husband worked at the same company. We agreed that it would be best if I found a job elsewhere."

At the end of the interview, the executive said, "There's just one area that I'm not clear on. You mentioned going through a divorce, though I don't know much about the issues between you and your former husband. Could you fill me in on that?"

The interview ended soon after this question. The candidate wrote a letter of complaint to the CEO and declined any further contact with the company. Ten months of work had been wasted. The company was grateful to not have been sued.

4. Invest your resources wisely. The first interview should be brief. It is essentially a first look for you and for the applicant. You must decide whether this person shows promise; if so, it is worth having them interviewed by others. On the other hand, if this is someone who you are confident will not fit, tell the person so.

I was asked to evaluate a candidate to supervise a group of managers. The mood among this group was toxic. There was a lot of destructive rivalry and nasty politics. Two previous incumbents had failed. Whoever took the job would have to gain loyalty by demonstrating their ability to be tough minded but fair.

The candidate had only very modest experience as a direct supervisor and no experience at this level. I told her that

*it would be unfair to expect that she could do this job. We
ended the interview after about thirty minutes.*

5. Take careful notes. I strongly recommend that you take careful
notes as the interview is unfolding. (This is yet another reason for
the structured interview. You know what's coming next, and you
avoid scrambling around trying to think up the next question.)

What works well is having two people conduct most interviews.
Using a structured interview technique means that you can divide
the questions roughly in half. One person asks the questions in
the first half while their interview partner takes notes (and doesn't
butt in). At the halfway mark, you switch roles. If done properly,
you put the two sets of notes together and have a reasonable tran-
script of what was asked and the answers that were given.

Having a written record allows the selection panel to have facts
they can point to. Without contemporaneous notes, the panel will
be left with incomplete, fragmented memories. These will be impressions rather than facts.

What do you write down? The most powerful information you
can record is a direct quote. This is infinitely better than writing
something like "seemed a bit nervous."

Do not record anything that is derogatory about the person. (If
you have a scribe, that person will have to be trained in what data to
capture.)

6. The key to understanding is listening. All good interviewers
have one thing in common. Without exception, they are good lis-
teners. You should be speaking no more than about 20 percent of
the time. You should be listening 80 percent of the time. I mean
really listening, which goes well beyond just hearing.

The words that are chosen convey about 8 percent of the meaning received by the listener. The rest of the communication is conveyed through voice quality, facial expression, body language, and a host of other nonverbal variables.

> **The way in which the interview is opened will dramatically influence how successful it is.**

A television journalist was interviewing a very senior politician. As he tried to direct the conversation, the interviewer said, "I ask the questions on this program." Without the ability to see or hear the exchange, it's impossible to know what was being communicated.

In seeing and hearing the conversation, however, it was immediately obvious that the two were friends. The comment was made with a warm smile. The politician responded with a matching smile and a gracious acceptance that he couldn't run the interview.

Listening with intent means a commitment to focus on grasping the underlying meaning, not just the words that are spoken. Now let's look at the questions to ask and how to ask them.

• • •

A SIMPLE SUMMARY

You catch more flies with honey than with vinegar.

CHAPTER 7

ADVANCED INTERVIEW CONCEPTS

You can't teach employees to smile.
They have to smile before you hire them.

—Art Nathan, president and COO of Strategic Development Worldwide

H ere we discuss the best questions to ask. (Some readers may have turned to this chapter first. You know who you are. There's always someone who wants to rush ahead.)

Keep in mind that there are no "best" questions. There are some that tend to work better than others and some that are just bad. Most commonly, these are the ones that tip the applicant to the answer you're looking for.

The questions that follow are simply ones that I have found helpful. In volume 3, I'll give you a wide variety of questions that are tailored for different jobs.

What follows is a fairly short, concise interview that can be adapted for a variety of roles. Depending on the age of the applicant, this format can include asking about time at school as well as past work history. I'll include tips on each of these.

OPENING THE INTERVIEW

The way in which the interview is opened will dramatically influence how successful it is. To quickly develop rapport, it's important to put yourself in the candidate's place. (Remember, you read about rapport in the last chapter. Oh, skipped that, did you? It's never too late.) A good introduction will consider the questions the candidate has and then answer them during the opening.

> **The candidate will undoubtedly tell other people about their experience with you. Good news travels fast, and bad news even faster.**

The purpose of this opening is to put the person at ease. It works. I've used this to begin several thousand interviews and have never had any problems.

This must be delivered in a conversational style. (If you're thinking of reading this to the candidate, please take a cold shower and think again.)

Opening the Interview	Guidelines for the Interviewer
Did you have any trouble locating our office? (Another icebreaker-type question, such as a comment about the weather, is equally suitable.)	This should be given only two to three minutes. This is simply a warm-up to help the candidate ease into the interview.
Thanks for your application and for coming in to meet with me today.	The candidate knows this is a requirement. Yet you don't want to pass up the opportunity to demonstrate that you are polite.
Before we get started, I'll tell you about what will happen today. I'd like to use the time we have to begin to get to know you.	You can be sure that this question is at the top of the candidate's mind.

You may find that some of the questions I'll ask will be a bit different from the ones you may have been asked at other interviews.	This is a very important cue. It means that when you get to the difficult questions, the applicant won't feel caught off guard.
Of course, if there is any question that you feel uncomfortable with, just let me know and we'll skip it. OK?	This lets the candidate know that they can elect to skip a question. (I've had only one person ask to do this.)
Does this raise any questions you'd like to ask?	These should be dealt with openly but briefly.
One more thing. You may be feeling a bit nervous. I think you'll find that as we talk, this will drop away.	This statement—said as if it's an afterthought—makes it normal to be nervous. Most often, the candidate does relax as the conversation unfolds.
The Job Opening	**Guidelines for the Interviewer**
To start, let's talk about the job we have open. I know it's early days, but what have you heard about this job so far?	Look for the following: • How much have they learned? • How assertively have they asked for information? (If the description is incomplete, give a concise overview to ensure that you and the applicant are speaking about the same job. Be brief. Resist the temptation to go into too much detail at this stage There will be time for this later.)
As closely as you can tell, what would be the main challenges that go with this job?	Has the candidate given any thought to this? How realistic is the candidate's assessment?
I know it is always hard to say with certainty, but from what you understand, what do you think you'd find most attractive about this job?	Consider how realistic this is. Will the candidate really get these rewards? Is the candidate looking to get away from a prior job or looking to join you?

Work History: Present Job	Guidelines for the Interviewer
Tell me about the job that you're doing now.	What does the candidate put first in their description? Often this will be what is most satisfying.
If you had to summarize the important features of this job in a couple of sentences, what would you say?	Look for how well they can synthesize their thoughts and boil down this longer subject to a few sentences.
How long have you been in this role?	Get the month and year of the start date.
What do you find most enjoyable about this job?	This will tell you a great deal about what could be enjoyable for the candidate and what they are looking for in a new job.
No job is perfect. What things have you found that are less enjoyable?	This, too, will give clues about what the candidate would prefer to avoid in a new job.
Leaving a job is always a pretty big decision. How did you decide to look for another role?	This is an important question and should be given sufficient time so that you understand the reasoning. Often a follow-up question will be needed. Insist that the candidate be as specific as possible.

Work History: Most Recent Jobs	Guidelines for the Interviewer
Review the candidate's three most recent jobs, using the same type of questions as for the candidate's present job. You will naturally need to reword the questions slightly so that you don't sound like a machine generating exactly the same question. Remember, you want to keep this conversational.	For each job, write down the date of starting, by month and year. Also write the name of the person they consider the supervisor or manager who knew them best.

School History	Guidelines for the Interviewer
This is particularly important for younger candidates. These are some of the areas you might want to find out about. How much detail you go into will depend on how long the person has been out of school.	Younger applicants have little or no real work experience. You must rely on clues that come from their schooling.

What is the last year level at school that you completed?	Did the candidate leave part way through a school year? If so, ask, "How did you decide to leave then?"
What clubs or teams did you join at school?	This reflects how sociable the candidate was. (This is less valid for people who had to work outside school hours.)
What subjects did you enjoy most at school? Enjoy least?	Look for any overlap of school subjects and sources of potential enjoyment at work.
Did you hold any part-time jobs during school?	Working during high school, especially if this was needed to help the family's finances, is an important clue about the early development of a work ethic. If someone comes from a stable financial background, not having worked isn't a negative.
Everyone tends to break the rules a bit in high school. What is the most significant example of you doing this?	Remember that this should be "the worst" example, independent of whether the candidate was detected.
Motivation	**Guidelines for the Interviewer**
Can you tell me about a time—a specific moment in time—when you felt a deep sense of satisfaction or accomplishment?	The answer will give you a window into what the candidate associates with pleasure. Will this job offer similar psychological rewards? It will also reveal values. There is a big difference between winning a sales competition and helping a colleague solve a problem.
Self-Confidence	**Guidelines for the Interviewer**
Can you tell me about some of the most significant risks you took in your last job?	Taking risks requires self-confidence tempered with good judgment. Study the answer here to assess both of these characteristics. Follow up with this question: "How did things work out?" Be sure to identify whether the risk was taken alone. Decisions made by a group require less self-confidence.

63

Resilience	Guidelines for the Interviewer
Life can bring a lot of different challenges. That's just the way it is. Can you tell me about a time when you felt most discouraged?	Insist on a specific moment in time rather than on a generic time period. Pay close attention to the source of the discouragement and how the candidate coped with this.
Dealing with Conflict	**Guidelines for the Interviewer**
We've all had to work with people who we didn't necessarily hit it off with. Can you tell me about a time when you were in this position?	Be alert for the candidate who will take the question to the extreme, saying that they've never had such a situation. Once identified, look at the core qualities of the answer. Consider how successful the outcome was and how the candidate achieved that result.
Emotional Intelligence	**Guidelines for the Interviewer**
Can you tell me about the last time you had a laugh at your own expense?	Most people will have little problem with this question. Be alert to those who struggle, who appear to not understand the question, or who give an example that seems like an answer but on closer inspection misses the mark.
Sometimes we must be able to read what another person is feeling, even if they don't say it directly. Can you describe a situation where you've had to do this?	Reading other people's feelings—often when they remain unspoken—is a large part of emotional intelligence. The follow-up question should be *"What was the outcome?"*
Self-Control	**Guidelines for the Interviewer**
We can all sometimes feel a bit frustrated at work. Tell me, when was the last time you lost your temper at work?	Many candidates will say that they've never lost their temper at work. For those who do give an example, consider their attitude to having done so and the cause of their anger.
Tell me about the time that you came closest to losing your temper at work.	This is a far more challenging question. Everyone should be able to give an answer.

Uncovering Developmental Needs	Guidelines for the Interviewer
We've all been in the situation of learning by experience. Looking back over your life, what would you say have been the three most important lessons you have learned?	This is a difficult question and requires some self-reflection. Without the follow-up question, it doesn't sound like it leads to a discussion of weakness.
Those all sound like good things to have learned. Can you take me through each one and tell me exactly how you learned that lesson?	This often will lead to a discussion of significant mistakes the candidate has made.
Think about the person in your life who is your toughest critic. *If I spoke with this person, and they were really going to be honest with me, how would they describe you?*	Pause to be sure that a particular person has been identified. Do not accept only a list of positives.
Technical Skills	**Guidelines for the Interviewer**
Think about all the things you've learned. Can you tell me about the three skills that you feel most proud of having learned?	This shifts the mood of the interview from mistakes to successes. It also opens up the topic of skills. Knowing which ones the candidate is most pleased to have learned will give you more insight into their character.

THE NEXT STEP

Thus far, the interview has focused on the candidate's character and values. The next step is to find out about the person's skills as they relate to the job summary. The very last question starts off this transition.

To assess skills, you must go beyond the candidate's self-report. Here is where the skills demonstration and the audition technique will be very helpful. Be sure that there is an objective scoring system for each of these exercises. This will be important when you try to compare the responses of two or more applicants. Volume 2 will describe how to do this in more detail.

. . .

A SIMPLE SUMMARY

The interview can reveal a wealth of information about the candidate. Remember to remain cautious. Even when skillfully conducted, the interview will give just a glimpse of the real person behind the interview mask.

CHAPTER 8

CHECKING REFERENCES

*I'd rather interview fifty people and not hire anyone than hire the
wrong person.*
—Jeff Bezos, founder and CEO of Amazon

R eference checking takes considerable skill to do well. The
main obstacle is that references are almost uniformly positive. The challenge is how to get past the referee's pat answer.

Perhaps this is why it is done poorly most of the time. It also
comes at the end of a lengthy process, and everyone just wants to
get to a conclusion. Under these circumstances, it can easily become a tick-the-box exercise.

> *The usual hiring cycle for fire brigades lasts between six to
> twelve months. These are very labor-intensive exercises.*
>
> *For one of our clients, reference checking was done during
> the meeting when final hiring decisions were being made.
> A phone call was placed by the receptionist, who then asked
> four rote questions. The most cursory of notes was made,
> often consisting of one or two words. (If the referee couldn't
> be immediately contacted, no follow-up was made.)*

*She would then report to the hiring committee, "The refer-
ence check is fine." (I never heard of a reference check that
wasn't fine.)*

*The only value I could see was that someone could put a
tick next to a box labeled "Reference check completed."*

ARRANGING THE REFERENCE
CHECK TELEPHONE CALL

Let the candidate contact the referees you want to speak with.
This doesn't stop you from independently speaking to other
referees that you may choose to contact yourself. Give the
candidate a schedule over the next week when you'd be free to
speak to a referee. Ask them to try and match the times the
referee is free with one of the time slots you've given. In some
cases you may have to be available before or after the usual
working hours. Note how quickly and ef-ficiently the candidate
manages to get this done.

Although you may be given the direct line to the candidate's
of-fice, always call the switchboard number. This lets you ensure
that the person you are calling actually works at that company.

UNDERSTANDING THE DYNAMICS
OF A REFERENCE CHECK

The person giving the reference has mixed loyalties. Sure,
they don't want to mislead you, a prospective employer, but the
person they're speaking about is well known to them, and
usually that's where the stronger loyalty lies.

Even when someone has been fired, their boss doesn't want to be the person who keeps them from getting another job. If you have any hope of getting useful data, this dynamic must be recognized and, where possible, overcome.

This is a structured interview. You must have a specific list of questions and a place to make notes of what you have been told.

OPENING THE PHONE CALL

Just as with the interview (and this is another type of interview), much will depend on how you open the call.

After introducing yourself and explaining why you are calling, tell the person that you expect the call to take about fifteen minutes. If this is an inconvenient time, it is up to you to be flexible. Often this means an early-morning call, before the day begins.

Set up the context of the job the candidate is applying for by explaining what it's like to work at your organization. Here's an approach that can be helpful.

> *Thanks for taking the time to speak with me. We'll probably need about fifteen minutes. Is this a convenient time? (If it isn't, you will need to reschedule.) I'd like to tell you a little bit about the job that Fred is applying for. We have a pretty tough, performance-based culture. In this role, Fred will be responsible for managing a sales territory. His compensation will start off on pure salary, but after a three-month training period, it will move to 80 percent salary and 20 percent commission. Our product line is high quality and therefore expensive. The biggest challenge is to fight off*

competitors who make products that look similar to ours but are sold much more cheaply.

We need your help. Fred looks like a promising candidate. On the other hand, we don't want to do him the disservice of placing him in a job that isn't right for him and where he'll struggle.

Would you mind if I asked you a few questions about your time working with Fred?

In some cases, it can help tip the referee's loyalty if you can say that the job in question is particularly challenging. If it is true, you may decide to tell the referee that your organization is very demanding, and if the candidate doesn't make the grade, it is likely that he will be terminated in three to six months. An important caution applies here. This method must be used judiciously. Avoid making the job harder than it really is, or your company being less tolerant than it is.

TEN IMPORTANT QUESTIONS TO ASK REFEREES

1. *What were the accountabilities this person was expected to meet?* Try to get specifics, and do not accept generalizations. Focus on what the person alone was responsible for. Commonly, people will say they were accountable for obtaining a certain end result, but on checking, you find that they were one of a team who shared this accountability, or perhaps it was their boss who had the final responsibility.

2. *How was overall performance measured?*

3. *To what extent did this person meet those targets?*

4. *How much independence to make decisions or spend money did this person have?* (Someone may say he was accountable for a budget of $100,000, but you discover that expenditures over $10,000 had to be approved by a supervisor.)

5. *What led to this person leaving the company?* (Notice the difference between this question compared to this one: *Why did this person leave?*)

6. *What do you think would have happened had this person remained in your employment?*

7. *Did you ever have to consider talking with this person about lifting their performance?*

8. *Roughly, how much sick leave did this person take?*

9. *Was there any behavior you were aware of—or heard about from others—that concerned you?*

10. *Would you hire this person again, without any reservations?* (This question needs to be asked verbatim.) Look for the person who pauses before answering or who is tentative in responding. "I would hire them again in a heartbeat!" is very different from "Let me see, I suppose I probably would."

To close off the conversation, you can ask "Speaking off the record, is there anything else I should know about Fred?" The phrase *off the record* sometimes encourages people to be more candid. Often, you'll find this last question to be very revealing.

GATHERING ADDITIONAL DATA

If the referee is vague or otherwise unhelpful, you might ask if there is anyone else in the organization who worked with the candidate and who you could talk to. Generally, you will be referred to someone else. (Don't bother talking to coworkers. You want to speak to someone who had a supervisory relationship with the applicant.) This second person will not have been handpicked by the applicant. It is unlikely that they will have the same loyalty as the selected referee.

> *In one case, a client had received a sterling reference about a candidate. However, my assessment showed some pretty substantial weaknesses. My client spoke to the previous employer and requested an introduction to someone else in the company. This new referee said that the candidate had been fired (this having been disguised so far) and was regarded as a liar and a cheat. None of that information came through from the handpicked referee.*

SEVEN GUIDELINES FOR REFERENCE CHECKING

1. Always check references thoroughly. There will be the occasional applicant who makes such a positive impression that you (or someone else) says, *"Let's skip the reference checking. This person's experience just screams success. They'll be great, but we better move quickly."* This is the time that you absolutely *must* do a thorough reference check.

2. Reference checking must be done by someone directly involved in the hiring process. It cannot be delegated to anyone else.

3. Always insist on references from three past direct supervisors. References from friends and coworkers are usually a complete waste of time.

4. Be sure to find out the relationship between the two people. Avoid leading questions, such as *"I understand that Susan reported directly to you."* It is preferable to ask the person their job title and the title of the job that your prospective hire was working in. Then you can ask, *"What was Fred's reporting relationship when at your company?"*.

5. Never settle for only a written reference. People find it easier to give glowing reports in a letter but tend to be more candid in a phone call.

6. Checking degrees and qualifications should be done as a matter of policy. Most people practice the art of résumé

inflation—at least a bit. There are some who carry this beyond what is considered acceptable. This includes making a claim to qualifications that are not genuinely held. Checking qualifications is a good way of assessing a candidate's honesty. Calling the institutions from which the person claims to have a qualification is a simple task that can be delegated to a junior person. It shouldn't be overlooked and can be started midway through the hiring cycle.

7. Look for a reluctance or hesitance to make a firm commitment. Also listen for what isn't said. (Consider what sentiment you might feel if you had fired someone who you basically liked.)

REFERENCES FROM YOUR COMPETITOR

Maintain a certain skepticism if the candidate is coming to your organization from one of your competitors. It's hard to fire people. How much easier it is to have them resign. Even better is to have them work for you!

> **Reference checking comes at the end of a lengthy process. Everyone just wants to get to a conclusion. Under these circumstances it can easily become a "tick the box" exercise.**

A not uncommon strategy is to send a competitor a problem person dressed up as a star performer. In one situation, I saw someone fired for incompetence. When he applied for a job in the same industry, the competitor who was thinking of hiring the person was given a glowing reference.

MEETING THE REFEREE

You may decide to meet the referee in person. You will often get far more information meeting someone in person than talking over the phone. This opportunity will present itself less frequently, but if you keep your eyes open, you will be surprised at how often it can be arranged. Sometimes you will have occasion to be in the same building where the referee works. You can say, after talking briefly on the phone, "I'll be near your office next Tuesday on some other business. Would you mind if I just dropped in for a couple of minutes around lunchtime?" While you are there, look for an opportunity to be introduced to anyone else who knew the person.

. . .

A SIMPLE SUMMARY

Reference checking is an extremely important part of the process. Avoid the temptation to take shortcuts here. When done well, this can turn up very worthwhile information.

CHAPTER 9

THE ROLE OF INTUITION

Intuition is always right in at least two important ways. It is always in response to something. It always has your best interest at heart.

—Gavin de Becker, American author and security specialist

I ntuition—or gut feeling, if you like—is critically important in making hiring decisions. The challenge is knowing what it is and how to use it.

INTUITION DEFINED

Knowing something by intuition means that we seem to know something without evidence. We arrive at a conclusion without the experience of conscious reasoning. Somehow, the idea or solution just seems to pop into our mind.

WHERE DOES IT COME FROM?

Something we know by intuition seems to come from nowhere. Actually, it arises from our mind being able to quickly—almost instantaneously—compare one experience with many others from our past.

> **It's critically important to separate impressions from facts.**

Here's an example. You are walking alone in the city at night. You see someone approaching you on the other side of the street. This person immediately gives you the impression of someone who is tough and potentially aggressive. You feel frightened. Sound familiar?

How do we know all this about a person at just a glance?

With time, we could look at a whole range of cues that this person is giving off. The way they are dressed, their style of walking, the look in their eyes, and a thousand other subtle hints are all read instantaneously by your unconscious mind. Would you disregard your intuition? Probably not.

What is very likely happening is that your mind is doing an instant comparison to a wide range of other people you have met over many years. Your mind sifts through this group and lands on some people who all have something in common: they caused you to feel anxious or afraid.

This can work in reverse. Have you ever met someone who you were immediately drawn to? They just seem to exude a sense of warmth and kindness. You felt you wanted to get to know them better. Here again, your unconscious mind is doing an instant comparison to others you've met.

SUSPICIONS ABOUT INTUITION

Some people view emotions and intuition as fallible, even whimsical, tools. These insights shouldn't be trusted, because they don't rely on facts. There is no scientific basis for this conclusion.

Intuition or gut feelings are the result of a lot of processing that happens in the brain to try to predict what is likely to happen in the future. The brain constantly compares incoming information against stored knowledge and memories of previous experiences. The goal is to predict what will come next.

When you have a lot of experience in a certain area, the brain has more information to match the current experience against. This makes your intuition more reliable. This means that your intuition can improve with experience. (That's why it is preferable to have staff doing selection to stay in the role to build up experience.)

USING INTUITION IN HIRING DECISIONS

A panel of police officers had been trained to select candidates. They found one candidate who they all felt had to be advanced to hiring. Yet all were uncomfortable with this decision. They called me. The chair of the panel explained that they felt stuck: "There was just something we couldn't put our finger on."

I asked how they pictured it would be driving in a patrol car with this person for an eight-hour shift. The mutual groans from everyone provided a clue. With encouragement, they all described how unpleasant it would be. "This guy would be talking all the time. He'd have to tell you how great he was at everything." In a dangerous situation, "He'd be at the back end of the car, telling you he needed a bathroom break."

The theme emerged of this being a self-centered person who would be a very poor team player and who could endanger others' safety.

What happened here is that the officers wanted to be as fair as possible. The candidate looked good on the external criteria. As the officers had only recently been trained, they were still learning to "read" applicants through interview data. The fact that none of them liked the applicant didn't seem relevant. In fact, that intuition proved to be the critical piece to unlocking the correct decision. This allowed the panel, with some help from me, to go over the other data we had. A range of other clues emerged that suggested this person would be difficult to get along with.

Making a hiring decision on gut feeling alone is not using these data properly. It's like sensing a pleasant smell coming from a nearby restaurant. Based on this, you decide to order that meal. This is justified because "it smells good."

Intuition is a powerful aid if you understand what it is and how to use it. It also requires a diligent search for other clues that can confirm or rebut what your intuition is telling you.

TWO POWERFUL QUESTIONS TO ASK ABOUT YOUR GUT FEEL

Having an intuitive hunch is fine, but how do you make it useful? This is often the problem when a committee tries to make a hiring decision. Usually, someone will say "I don't know what it is, but I'm uncertain about this candidate," In other words, my gut is telling me something but I don't know what it is.

Try these two questions. It's very important that you respond with whatever immediately comes to mind.

1. **Would I want this person to work with, or for, someone who I really cared about?**

    •   How would they get along with the person I love?

    •   How would they handle conflict with this person?

    •   Would this person willingly "go the extra mile" when necessary?

    •   How much direction or support would they need?

    •   How would they cope with negative feedback about their performance?

    •   If given an unpleasant assignment, what will their likely reaction be?

2. **Assume you know how to sail a boat. You're starting off on a cruise that will take about twenty-four hours. It will be dark as you sail home. There is no way to predict with certainty the weather or roughness of the sea. The boat requires a crew of twelve. You have selected all but one. You are considering asking this candidate to join the crew.**

    •   How will this person get on with the other crew?

    •   Would this person carry their share of the workload?

- Would this person accept responsibility for their mistakes?

- Does this person show a reasonable level of confidence in their ability while retaining a sense of modesty?

- How will they act when things don't going to plan?

- How will they react to taking orders in an emergency situation?

Now, with this insight, review the data you already have. It may support your intuition or may argue against it. Then the task is to use all of what you know about this person to make a hiring decision.

• • •

A SIMPLE SUMMARY

Intuition is critically important. It is even more powerful when you know how to translate it into specific hunches about how a person will act at work. Always look for objective data to confirm or refute your intuition.

CHAPTER 10

MAKING THE FINAL DECISION

People are not your most valuable asset. The right people are.
—**Jim Collins, author of** *Good to Great*

The next step in the selection process is to gather all the available information to form a hiring decision. If the earlier steps have been followed, this part should be reasonably straightforward. To the extent that shortcuts were taken, or areas skipped, more imagination will be required. I use the word *imagination* deliberately. When you don't have the data, the best you can do is imagine what it might look like if you did have it.

WHY PEOPLE SUCCEED AT WORK

People succeed largely because their personalities and values match the job and the culture. It is rare that someone becomes a poor performer because of a lack of skills. It is this value match that is so critical to evaluate before making a hiring decision.

NINE REQUIREMENTS FOR PEOPLE WHO STAFF
A RECRUITMENT PROCESS

1. These staff should have a demonstrated history of managing confidential information.

2. These staff should have an excellent level of skill in reading people.

3. It is critical that these staff have a clear commitment to selecting only the most appropriate candidate. They need some skin in the game.

4. A degree of independence in thinking combined with appropriate levels of courage should be present while also excluding those who disagree just for the sake of it.

5. Each person on the selection panel should have had professional training in how to select staff. (Junior staff who join the selection panel must have completed formal training and been coached by more experienced staff.)

6. These staff should be able to use instinctual judgment while also supplying the reasons for their conclusions.

7. These staff should have practice in executing the structured hiring decision model you use. (You do have one by now, don't you?)

8. These staff will need to appreciate the importance of personality in making a selection decision and not be blinded by credentials alone.

9. All staff will need to be excellent team players.

You should allow as many visits to your office as are necessary to form a firm opinion. Let people interview in pairs so that one can take notes while the other poses questions. The roles can be reversed halfway through the interview. The value of this approach is that different people will get a different take on the interviewee.

Use multiple interviews to arrange at least one meeting outside the office. Lunch is an excellent time to observe a candidate. You will often see different aspects of a person's character when you change the setting.

> *A financial services firm wanted to hire a CEO. The best candidate was identified through a search firm. During several interviews, his performance was as smooth as polished glass. Those who met him were struck by his charm and diplomatic manner. However, at a lunch interview, it immediately became obvious that this person could be grossly insensitive. He was both arrogant and rude to the waitstaff. Even more interesting was a complete lack of awareness that this behavior was at all unusual.*

Remember the importance of having subordinates to the role included in the assessment panel. I appreciate that having subordinates involved in the decision may be controversial in some places. The only explanation for this that I have found is that somehow this gives too much power to the subordinates. This makes little sense to me. They will be only one part of the hiring decision, but they will have to live with this person. Unless this group is very dysfunctional, I can see little downside and much upside to including subordinates in the process.

We all tend to see life through our own filters. No one will bring pure objectivity. You are looking for two things from all the interviewers: any hint of a red flag that

> **Having an intuitive hunch is fine, but how do you actually make it useful? It is usually unpersuasive to tell an applicant you didn't get the job "because we had a hunch!"**

hasn't been picked up so far and their estimate of the fit between the applicant and the firm.

Oh yes, one more thing. This approach takes time. Considered as an investment and a risk management strategy, this will be a small cost to getting the right person.

PRACTICAL STEPS TO GUIDE YOUR HIRING DECISIONS

Step 1: Identify seven sources of facts. It's critically important to know whether a piece of data is a fact or an impression. A failure to distinguish between these is often at the heart of many hiring mistakes.

What makes a fact so useful is that often it will be the exact words written down by one of the interviewers as the candidate spoke them. Seven types of facts will be available.

- *Observations of Staff Who Spoke to the Candidate by Phone*

    A male applicant to a police agency phoned the recruit-ment area. When a woman answered the call, saying "This is Senior Sergeant Jones…" He immediately said, "Look, sweetie, I need to speak with the top guy there." She qui-etly explained that she was head of recruitment and asked how could she help him. This comment was recorded in a behavioral observation form. If this man were advanced to interview, that would have been part of his file.

- *A Direct Quote from the Applicant*

No one can capture everything that is said by an applicant. The amount of weight to be placed on any one comment will range dra-matically. In every interview, there are some comments that stand out as being so unique that they just beg for attention.

    An applicant described their work background as being "pretty consistent, as I've always been in the computer in-dustry." Asked about their style of management, this person said, "Some people who have worked for me would say that my style is a lot like Hitler's. Nah, I was only joking."

Clearly these two quotes should be given different weightings. The first is almost a platitude. The second is highly revealing, quite idiosyncratic, and certainly worthy of follow-up.

- *A Behavioral Observation Describing How the Candidate Dressed for the Interview*

Many years ago, I was asked to evaluate a candidate for a senior executive position. He came to the interview dressed in a sport coat, slacks, and rather snappy loafers. What struck me most was his choice to wear an ascot. At that time (long before we had casual dress days), this was commonly worn exclusively by movie stars. The overall impression was of someone who didn't feel a need to conform to the usual business uniform of a suit and necktie. There were several signs in the interview to support the impression of someone who needed to feel special.

During the interview, when describing his strengths, he spoke at some length about his ability to build cohesive teams. Some months later, I was speaking with one of his subordinates. She complained that when traveling, he sat in business class while the team rode in economy.

- *A Behavioral Observation of What the Candidate Did During the Interview*

This can be an observation both of what the candidate did and what they failed to do that would be considered appropriate.

During the opening of an interview with an executive candidate, I explained that I might be interrupted for a brief phone call. The call did come through. When I had to make a short note and found that I had nothing to write with, he quickly passed over a pen. I was struck by his courtesy. After

I hung up, he made a sarcastic remark that had a sting to it. This brief interaction gave two different impressions of his character.

- **A Written Note of How the Applicant Dealt with the Demands of the Interview Situation**

Some years ago, I had an office in a building that had been converted from a home. From my office window, I would occasionally hear the neighbors speaking. On this occasion, several members were having a loud and volatile argument, yelling at the top of their voices. This lasted about fifteen minutes.

The candidate I was interviewing did not show even the slightest sign of interrupted concentration. Her explanations were clear, relevant, and to the point. She gave no indication that she was even aware of the noise (though it would have been impossible to not be aware of it.)

- *Observations of Staff Who Interacted with the Candidate Outside the Interview*

I happened to notice an applicant in our office treating my assistant in a very perfunctory way. His manner was just short of being rude. I later checked with that staff member to get her impressions. She said that he behaved this way during her entire interaction with him. This was in sharp contrast to the charm he exhibited with me. She had already made a written observation about this behavior, complete with quotes.

- *A Test Score, When Available*

This assumes, of course, that the test has been properly selected, administered and scored. If tests are to be used, the organization must be extremely diligent in ensuring that each of these steps are carried out with precision.

Step 2: **Identify rule-out factors.** There are certain factors that argue strongly against hiring someone regardless of what other positives there may be. The most obvious of these is lacking a required qualification. If you are legally required to have someone who is a registered nurse, nothing will take the place of meeting this standard.

There are also certain personality traits that can be so disruptive that they will outweigh a group of positive factors. For well over thirty-five years, I've been giving workshops to teach people to evaluate job applicants. In most cases, I ask the group to think of someone they have worked with (or for) who was a clear hiring mistake. They are then encouraged to describe how this person behaved that made them a poor choice.

The Dirty Dozen: Twelve Rule-Out Factors
These are twelve characteristics that come up in every discussion.

1. *Lazy:* This person looks for the easiest way to get the job done. They are happy to cut corners.

2. *Blames others:* When things go wrong, it is always someone else's fault.

3. *Unable to accept negative feedback:* In their own mind, this person is always right. No matter what errors are observed, there is always a reason why someone else should be blamed.

4. *Unable to follow instructions:* This person insists on doing things their own way and can rarely follow a basic procedure.

5. *A loner:* This person has trouble getting along with others most of the time. The few people they do get along with (sort of) are staff with the same bad habits they have.

6. *Authoritarian:* This person never asks nicely. They can only feel comfortable bossing people around.

7. *Self-centered:* This person lives by the following motto: "We've been talking about me long enough. Let's talk about you and what you think about me."

8. *Dishonest:* This person lacks integrity. They are happy to steal from their employers or to blatantly lie about their behaviors, motives, or almost anything else that will make them look good.

9. *Impulsive:* This person lives by the motto of "Ready, fire, aim."

10. *Arrogant:* This person acts superior to others. They expect to be given certain privileges without having earned them. They will avoid jobs that are "beneath them."

11. Lacks common sense: For this person, common sense—the ability to share a perception that almost everyone would have—can be very hard to find.

12. Severe Personality Problems: This can range from behavior that is extremely quirky and unusual to suffering from serious problems. These can include problems managing mood, disruptive levels of anxiety or substance abuse problems.

Now that you know about the dirty dozen, which of these would make someone unsuitable to be hired where you work? What if the person demonstrated two of these traits, or even three?

> **Often you have to rely on intuition. Bill Gates, Founder of Microsoft**

Most such applicants would have been ruled out earlier in the process. However, occasionally someone can go through to reference checks and final interviews before a rule-out decision is made. What is needed here is courage (with a capital C!). If something is discovered at this late stage that leads to a rule-out decision, it will take real courage to avoid the trap of persisting with the person despite obvious warnings.

Step 3: Distinguish impressions from facts. An impression is an idea or belief about someone. These can often be a bit vague, and even the source of the impression can be hard to pin down. There is no objective reference to which the impression can be linked.

For example, noting that the candidate seemed to lack confidence may be valuable, but until it can be linked to some objective reference, it remains only an impression. Concluding that this person "would be an excellent team member" is an impression only, until it has some supporting data.

Step 4: Create a list of facts and a separate list of impressions. This list should be a summary of all the data that has been gathered.

Step 5: Refer to the job summary that was created early in the process. Review each component and make a list of facts or impressions that support the decision to hire and those that would recommend against hiring this person. This list of data should be organized against the key selection criteria.

Step 6: Consider what the risk is if the wrong person is hired. Given what you know (and you will never know everything), what would you estimate the chances are of this being a suitable hiring decision? Use a scale of 1 to 10, where 1 equals severe doubt that it will be a correct decision, and 10 equals absolute confidence that the candidate will be at least an average performer.

Step 7: Consider the annual salary for this job. Now add 10 to 20 percent for overhead. Multiply that number by 6. For a salary of $70,000, we have overhead of, say, $14,000. Multiply this by 6. Thus, your minimum investment is $504,000.

Step 8: Consider your investment. If this were your company, would you be happy to write a check to this person for that amount? (If this person is hired, someone will.)

Step 9: Consider the effect on the business, your team, and your reputation if you get it wrong. Will this person fully support both the immediate tactical challenges and the longer-term vision of the company? How will your team feel about this new hire? Have they had any input into the hiring decision? How will a hiring mistake affect the way your bosses judge your management skills? What about your peers?

All this information should help you to make a decision that will be as close to objective as possible.

TWO TRAPS TO BE AWARE OF

There are two common traps that await you at this final stage. Each can be quite seductive, and both need to be understood and resisted.

1. The Panel Decision Trap

This is where there is some agreement, whether stated or not, that the majority vote of the panel will make the hiring decision. Another version of this trap is when the vote of the panel chair is given more weight than other panel members.

What's the problem? This happens when one person on the panel picks up something about the candidate that others haven't identified. This reservation about a candidate cannot be overcome by a majority vote. What's needed is a careful analysis of the basis for the concern about hiring the person.

The final decision should occur only when the entire panel is in agreement. (Getting agreement by bullying the dissenter, or by pulling rank, is a formula for a bad decision.)

2. The Formula Trap

Some people advocate for having a scoring system. The most basic form is assigning points to each interview question. (It can get a lot more complex. Putting someone on the panel who leans toward being obsessive-compulsive will give you a scoring matrix that will require a degree in statistics to understand!)

> *A client asked for our help in selecting a candidate for a unique job situation. Two people had been selected over the last few years. Both failed dramatically. We were told, "We just can't afford another mistake."*

> *Our team designed a selection methodology. When reviewing it with our client, the chair said, "I'm so relieved that you aren't trying to score every question." This is what had been done in the past, amid much disagreement.*

> *The client was part of the public service. This scoring method had been introduced so that the decision would be objective and not based just on the opinions of one or more people.*

> *I asked our client what they did in the past. She said, "We followed the process and added up the scores, just as we were told." I then asked, "What happened if the scores didn't agree with what the panel wanted?" Without missing a beat, our client said, "Easy. We just went back and changed the scores."*

The problem here is that every hiring decision will be subjective. The methods in this book are designed to bring as much objectivity as possible, but there is no scoring system that can make this an objective decision.

. . .

A SIMPLE SUMMARY

Hiring decisions are always made by one or more people. Use as many methods as possible to add objective data. Despite this, it will always be an inherently subjective decision.

SOME CLOSING THOUGHTS

Nothing in the world can take the place of persistence. Talent will not: nothing is more common than unsuccessful people with talent. Genius will not: unrewarded genius is almost a proverb. Education will not: the world is full of educated derelicts. Persistence and determination alone are omnipotent.

—Calvin Coolidge, thirtieth president of the United States

By now, I hope that you have been convinced of the wisdom of approaching hiring in a thoughtful and systematic fashion. I also hope that I have persuaded you of the importance of understanding who a candidate really is before making a hiring decision. Let's suppose you want to introduce these ideas where you work.

TWO STEPS FOR INITIATING
A NEW HIRING PRACTICE

1. Gather objective data. If you work in human resources, this should be easy. If not, you may have to hunt around. It will be there somewhere. You want to know how many people were hired in a given time period, and how many of those would be considered a good hiring decision.

2. Calculate the costs of a hiring mistake.

- Cost of attraction strategy: This will include the cost of all the internal meetings as well as money spent on advertising or agency fees.

- Cost of selection: The time of the interview panels working on the selection, reference-checking time, and meetings to make a decision.

- Cost of induction and training.

- Cost of separation: Legal fees, payouts to employee, and staff time staff taken up with these matters.

- Business impact: Effect on customers, on staff morale, and on suppliers.

- The cost of replacing good staff who have left.

- Opportunity cost: What would our business look like if we had chosen an average performer who got the job done and who got along with us?

- Cost of starting over to replace this person.

THREE COMMON EXAMPLES OF RESISTANCE

At first, most people will appear to welcome ideas that lead to better hiring decisions. But people are attracted to what is comfortable. Doing things in a new way can be challenging. Typically, you'll find some people in the organization more open to these ideas while others are opposed, sometimes vigorously. Here are three responses you may hear.

1. "I don't need this."

Most people are attracted to what is familiar. Doing things in a new way can be confronting. People feel anxious about change. They worry that they won't be able to learn something new or that the change might reflect badly on them.

> One of our clients hired people to be in charge of troubled teenagers living in group homes. One manager had a terrible reputation for consistently hiring unsuitable people. When the notion of introducing a more rigorous hiring system was introduced, she strongly resisted. When her hiring mistakes were raised, all could be explained away by factors having nothing to do with her. Ultimately, it became so difficult to get agreement that a decision was made to introduce changes while specifically telling her that she was not required to participate. Although she was the most vocal, there were other managers who quietly expressed the same reservations.
>
> This could easily look like a loss for people who wanted change. At our suggestion the client saw an opportunity for a mini experiment. A committee member simply kept track of the number of people hired by each manager. The

measures of hiring success previously outlined were collected and tallied.

2. "I've had so much experience that this will be a waste of my time."
This statement is based on the assumption that with more experience one gets better at making hiring decisions. Unfortunately, experience does not necessarily equate to getting better at a task. Indeed, there is no objective support for this idea. This is particularly true when there is no way to formally measure the outcome of hiring decisions.

3. "This is going to take too long. I just don't have that much time available."
This is usually accompanied by expressions of urgency that *"we have to fill this job!"* This often reveals an unspoken view that hiring is a distraction from *"my real job"* and *"I can't spend too much time because I've got all this work to do."*

MANAGING RESISTANCE

I have had the least success when I tried to explain the reasons for a new approach. Usually, this invites the other party to come back with more arguments in favor of their position.

> **Remain alert to decisions made by "the majority" or suggestions that a scoring system will make "things more objective".**

SEVEN QUESTIONS
TO ASK THOSE WHO SEE NO NEED FOR CHANGE

1. In looking into our recruitment it looks like we get it wrong about one in four times. (fill in the numbers for your orga-nization.) Is that good enough?

2. Yes, it will take more time, but what happens if we get this wrong? How much time will that take?

3. If we make a bad hiring decision, how is that going to affect the way staff see us as managers?

4. Yes, I agree that this person seems to have the right skills and the right background. Is that enough for us to be sure that this person will be successful?

5. What assurance do we have that this person has the right character and personality traits to fit into our culture?

6. How confident can we be that this person's descriptions of their past performance and successes have been completely candid?

7. It does seem like this person has the right background, based on what they tell us. Is it possible that they may have exaggerated or even lied about their background?

It's also useful to have some spectacular hiring mistakes (if this has happened where you work) to refer back to.

Top management at a corrections agency wanted to have twenty recruits to fill a new trainee class. The recruitment team, having screened about four hundred applicants, found nineteen to be suitable. The answer from management was that "we never run a class for fewer than twenty people. It isn't cost effective. Get one more!"

One of the clerical staff members assisting on the project was told, "Go through the most recent reject list and see if anybody there might work." She soon came up with a person she described by saying, "I remember talking to him on the phone. He seemed like quite a good guy." That was enough for him to be hired.

After completing the training, he was sent to work in a maximum-security prison housing serious offenders. He was seduced into bringing in something very minor that prisoners wouldn't usually have access to. After doing this once, he fell victim to blackmail from the prisoners. They threatened to advise the authorities of what he had done, which would lead to instant dismissal. Over the next several months, he was induced to bring in candy and then cigarettes, leading up to phones and drugs.

On the next occasion, he was told to go to an address in the community. "Now, this guy is gonna give you a gun and some shells. You bring 'em to work tomorrow. We're gonna break outta this place."

Fortunately, the police learned about this through wiretaps on some known criminals. When this man came to work the next morning, he was arrested in the parking lot. Searching his car, police found a handgun, shells, and drugs. He was sentenced to five years in jail.

Naturally, the story became a legend in the organization. When the recruitment team was pressured to do things quickly, or to fill quotas for a class, they quietly referred to this incident. That was the end of the objection.

This clearly is an extreme case. However, hiring mistakes become legendary in most places. With some thought, anyone who has been employed for a while will have examples they can refer back to.

BE PERSISTENT

Sometimes it can be very hard to change perceptions. If you advocate for an improved hiring system and it isn't accepted, avoid getting upset; there will be more opportunities. As you begin to gather your own data about hiring mistakes, you will have much more leverage at your next attempt.

Meanwhile, congratulate yourself on gaining more insight into this critically important management role.

. . .

A SIMPLE SUMMARY

Change can take place in an instant, or it can take years. Perseverance is always the key. Timing is everything.

A REQUEST FOR A FAVOR

I hope that you have enjoyed reading this book. It has many tips and tricks to help you avoid the common hiring traps that are so easy to fall into.

You will also have lots of ideas about how to pick better people.

Now, I hope you won't mind if I ask a favor? Please take a minute and record your thoughts on an Amazon review.

Here's how: go the the book on Amazon. Scroll down the page and you'll see Product Description. Scroll further and you'll see Product Details. Below that you'll then see Leave a Review.

You might like to tell friends about this book, or notify people on your social media sites liked Facebook and LinkedIn.

And don't forget, as a purchaser of this book, you're entitled to a free additional chapter that I've written. Just drop me a note at www.drkenbyrne.com.

Reviews are very helpful, and I promise to read each one carefully. I'll use your feedback to make Volume 2 even better!

Thanks very much in advance for your support.

WHAT'S COMING IN VOLUME 2

How to Build Trust and When to Start

Using Social Media to Get the Attention of the Very Best Candidates

How to Write a Job Ad That Candidates Will Read

How to Create a Uniquely Attractive Culture

Using a Résumé to Gather Unconscious Clues About the Candidate

Powerful Listening Tools to Help Get Behind the Interview Mask

How to Use the Work Sample

Practical Tips for Using the Single Most Powerful Selection Method

More Powerful Questions to Assess the Candidate's Character

Five Types of People Who Should Never Be Hired

How to Elicit and Understand the Candidate's Most Important Values

Induction and Onboarding Done Right

Keeping the Stars You've Attracted

ACKNOWLEDGMENTS

I want to thank the following friends and colleagues who read early drafts of this book. Each has made very useful suggestions, and the book is better thanks to their input:

George Dingli

Jim McMahon

John Ross

Mike Ryan

Bob Wicks

Jeff Zeig

The observations of my wife, Diana, have been particularly insightful and helpful.

I'm grateful to have had the help of my assistant, Miranda Catanuso. She carried out the proofing, editing, and preparation of the final draft with her usual combination of attention to detail and sound practical judgment.

ABOUT THE AUTHOR

D r. Ken Byrne has been in full-time independent practice as a corporate psychologist since 1979. His clients have ranged from large multinationals to small businesses. Over the last forty years, he has personally evaluated more than three thousand job applicants ranging from candidates for CEO and other senior executive roles, middle management, technical roles and entry level staff.

In the mid-1980s, Dr. Byrne became interested in the selection challenges faced by public safety groups, such as police, fire brigades, ambulance, corrective services, and other similar organizations. This led to his developing a personality questionnaire designed specifically for public safety applicants. This allowed clients to screen large groups of people and then to use an empirically derived formula to rate the level of risk each applicant posed. Candidates the agency decided to advance to interview were further screened with a highly specialized series of interview tools.

In about 2005, Dr. Byrne became interested in the screening of people to work in aged care and disability services. This led him to develop a brief personality screening test and interview guides for applicants to these critical roles.

Dr. Byrne has also headed several research studies to validate and norm each of these specialized screening tools. This resulted in publication of numerous long-term follow-up studies of people who had been screened, comparing them to groups hired without this specialized assessment.

His experience and expertise in evaluating candidates has led to him being indirectly involved in hiring decisions of thousands of other people is in the broad public safety area.

Dr. Byrne completed Bachelor's and Master's degrees in Clinical Psychology and earned a Doctor of Psychology degree from Hahnemann Medical College in Philadelphia. He started in corporate psychology with the Hay Group in their Philadelphia head office before beginning his private consulting practice.

Dr. Byrne is well known for his lively, entertaining and informative talks and training seminars.

INDEX

.

www.ingramcontent.com/pod-product-compliance
Lightning Source LLC
Chambersburg PA
CBHW060611200326
41521CB00007B/732